Etsy Guide:

Etsy Business Lessons To Earn $1000 per Month

Copyright 2016 by publisher - All rights reserved.

This document is geared towards providing exact and reliable information in regards to the topic and issue covered. The publication is sold with the idea that the publisher is not required to render accounting, officially permitted, or otherwise, qualified services. If advice is necessary, legal or professional, a practiced individual in the profession should be ordered.

- From a Declaration of Principles which was accepted and approved equally by a Committee of the American Bar Association and a Committee of Publishers and Associations.

In no way is it legal to reproduce, duplicate, or transmit any part of this document in either electronic means or in printed format. Recording of this publication is strictly prohibited and any storage of this document is not allowed unless with written permission from the publisher. All rights reserved.

The information provided herein is stated to be truthful and consistent, in that any liability, in terms of inattention or otherwise, by any usage or abuse of any policies, processes, or directions contained within is the solitary and utter responsibility of the recipient reader. Under no circumstances will any legal responsibility or blame be held against the publisher for any reparation, damages, or monetary loss due to the information herein, either directly or indirectly.

Respective authors own all copyrights not held by the publisher.

The information herein is offered for informational purposes solely, and is universal as so. The presentation of the information is without contract or any type of guarantee assurance.

The trademarks that are used are without any consent, and the publication of the trademark is without permission or backing by the trademark owner. All trademarks and brands within this book are for clarifying purposes only and are the owned by the owners themselves, not affiliated with this document.

Table of content

Etsy Guide: 1
    Etsy Business Lessons To Earn $1000 per Month.......................................1
Introduction: Etsy Calling! 5

Chapter 1: What is Etsy? 7

Chapter 2: Building Your Etsy Empire!..9

Chapter 3: Developing a Client Base 17

Chapter 4: Make more than $1000 dollars a month 19

Conclusion: Thoughts on Prometheus 24

Introduction: Etsy Calling!

Many of us receive what we could call a calling in life and it was Etsy that gave me and my wife such a big boost later on in our own career. She was still busy with school and I was a recent graduate barely holding down a part time job at UPS, but then we found Etsy and with the added financial component that Etsy was able to provide to our income we were able to stay afloat. It was a niche that seemed especially perfect for us because she had always been into craft making and vintage goods and I had always been a very enthusiastic patron of DIY projects.

My wife is also a social media genius so partnering with her and utilizing that kind of prowess was crucial to lift our little idea up out of the corner of our mind and into the limelight of big business online marketing. And all of this was achieved in just a matter of months! Freelance contract work, and freelance shops and businesses are the wave of the future and they are rapidly changing the world and more importantly how we see commerce.

Last year self employed online business owners and contractors made up a very significant portion of the workforce and the new jobs that were created. A workforce revolution directly spurned on by the digital edge, and as the numbers are showing more and more people are stepping away from their stuffy nine to five day job in favor of trying something new. Many of us our now surprising ourselves to find that we have a new calling on life, with entrepreneurial opportunities like Etsy knocking right on our door.

And if you feel a true desire and passion to start your own business, take charge of your life and be your own boss, then why not? If you feel that you are a creative, intelligent person who knows what people need and how to give it to them, don't be shy. Take hold of your dream and your life! They say opportunity waits for no one, when we see a good fit for us in life we should run for it, so follow the guide set forth in this book and keep your ear to the ground because whether you are ready or not, Etsy is calling!

Chapter 1: What is Etsy?

Etsy began its life as an online arts and crafts bulletin board created by three art students from Brooklyn New York. This was during the first wave of hipster trendiness when Rob Kalin, a founding member took the idea to a whole knew level with the concept of creating what he termed as a new consumer "economy" that would reestablish bonds between buyer and seller and furthermore only the merchant involved to sell products that they had constructed themselves. Taking things all the way back to the feudal mercantile days of yester year this was a hipster's beaded necklace fantasy!

But not only does Etsy allow users to buy and sell vintage and hand made products. Etsy is also very intuitive and user friendly for anyone that wants to literally set up shop in their marketplace. Simulating a digital shopping center, buyers can design their own tailor made stores for whatever it is that they happen to be selling. And along with making items easy to sell they are streamlined in such a way that the experience of the buyer is greatly enhanced as well. And given item that you are seeking to purchase for Etsy is listed in the seller database and a simple typed query in the search engine will bring up exact matches of whatever it is that you are looking for.

The user friendly and innovation enabling features of platforms like Etsy owe much of their existence to the revolution 2.0 technologies which have enabled the average user to not only view they internet but to help them create platforms of their own. Beginning in 2002 this urge of self expression emerged as many new opportunities for self employment and by the time of the Recession of 2008 there was a full fledged boom of entrepreneurs buying and selling on marketing platforms such as Etsy.

Etsy, a name that is derived from the Italian phrase, "eh si" meaning "What If" first launched on June 18th 2005, but the first real sign that this thing was going to be big however came in 2009 when the up-cycling trend kicked it into high gear. This was the year that anything from clothing to furniture was being repurposed like mad and everyone was eager to jump on the up-cycled bandwagon. And when it came to reconditioned products, Etsy proved to be the perfect marketplace for their showcasing and purchasing.

Since the policy of Etsy is to only market vintage or handmade products (no new nikes allowed!" The world of up-cycled proved to be ripe for Etsy marketing. Before the up-cycling trend, Etsy was relegated to simply being a haven for odds and ends like beaded necklaces and tie-dyed shirts, basically all the items you expect to find at a flea market, but this digital flea market was greatly transformed when common industrial items such as pallets were being up cycled into everything from couches to guitars. This opened up a huge amount of possibilities under the auspice of "hand made" items.

As testament to this is what many have termed the grandma factor involved in the products that are sold on the site. Everything that you can find in your grandmothers basement is readily available on Etsy! All you have to do is just look for them! Etsy has revolutionized the way we buy and sell and if you want to know how you can hop aboard this revolutionizing gravy train, read on!

Chapter 2: Building Your Etsy Empire!

When beginning any kind of enterprise, proper planning is of the utmost importance. This is true whether your entrepreneurial base is lodged in a physical building somewhere of if it is placed in the online marketplace. For Etsy beginners you may be amused that the first fatal mistake that people make at the start is that they have no idea what it is that they are going to sell! It sounds comical, but this happens quite a bit!

It is the nature of the digital realm that makes it easy to commit to something even when you don't have the goods! Where it would be exceedingly rare for someone to buy or rent out an empty store front without anything to put into it! In the digital market though, no matter how user-friendly and easy the web application of it is, if you do not have a good item to market it is like you are utilizing a great new drill without having any drill bits! And while you are shooting blanks you are just ruining things for yourself and anyone else that has sites on real marketing.

So one great recommendation, if you do not have something that you are absolutely determined will make a killing in the market, the next best (and many times better) thing for you to do is to check out what everyone else is selling on Etsy. Keeping on eye out on the competitor has been the clear model for business acuity since business began. And one that is easy to understand, if you see that knitted socks are selling like hotcakes then contemplate making that your commodity, or if you see that it is up-cycled furniture that is being bought up like no tomorrow then you can contemplate getting into the up-cycling business.

Keeping an eye for what's hot among your competitors is a fundamentally simple key in the marketing business.

Another crucial thing to implement in your selling process is to take note of some of the rules that will be an integral part of your contract experience. So when you sign up for an Etsy account do not just scroll through all of the regulations in your user contract, read them, and not only read them, also print them out so that you have a physical copy to use as a reference at all times. The rules will also help to inform you on what it is that you can sell and what items are strictly off limit, so having these regulations easy to access is a good guide for you at any time.

When creating your Etsy account you will have to provide Etsy with a few details about yourself. Remember in business accountability is a good thing and the more of it you and your potential buyers provide the less chance of problems later on. First you will have to provide Etsy with your name. Simple enough right? And we all have one I assume? After this information has been provided you will ten have to submit to the system your own uniquely created username and password, these will be the two key identifiers that you will use to log into the Etsy system.

Once you are logged in for the first time you will ten receive a prompt to create a "shop name" for the platform that you will be selling your products under. New users often fail to realize how important that this step actually is, because the name that you choose will stick with you for life. Whatever name that Jane or John Doe chooses will be forever attached to them on their Etsy account. So please trail to make your shop name relevant and accurate for whatever it is that you are trying to sell on Etsy.

You should spend a good amount of time brainstorming a name, make the name reflect what it is that you want to do and also the majority of merchandise that you wish to sell through the system. If you are wanting to sell a wide variety of items keep your name as general and open to that as possible. If you are determined just to sell one type of product make the name reflect that as well. You should come up with a list of at least 5 good and relevant names and then search them on Etsy to make sure that they are not already in use. You don't want your name to be nearly identical to another either.

Having a name that is only different by one character may get you through the door but it will kill the potential of your future sales. Remember folks, this ain't yahoo and on Etsy if you see a shop named Pretty Flowers and you decide you like the name so much that you will be Pretty Flowers123 it will make you lose sales and your most precious resource of all; customers!

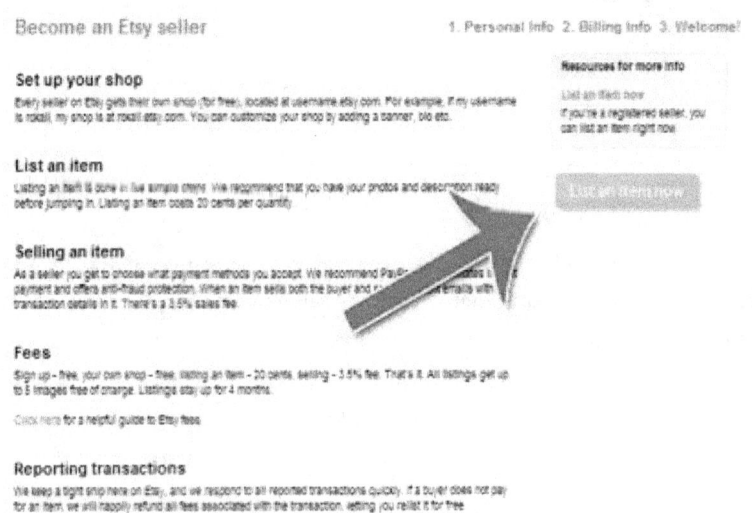

After the naming of your shop has been established you can then move on to the creation of your banner. The banner is of extreme importance to you and your potential buyer so please don't miss this important step. The banner is the first thing that any potential buyer will see on your site. According to the specifications on Etsy the banner must be 760 pixels wide and 100 pixels high and the resolution must be 72 dots per inch.

If you are not quite up on all your techie mumbo jumbo, then don't worry about it, because there is a device that you can utilize that will pretty much do everything for you Just take a peak at the "Etsy's Bannerator". Using this thing will generate some awesome banner designs for you for free. After your banner is setup the next thing that you need to take care of is setting up your own personal avatar or photo for your profile. This, just like your banner should be something that is eye catching and draws a particular buyer in, so try to scrounge up something that is good and relatable to an audience, so a word to the wise, that picture of you in that mustard stained t-shirt from Aunt Jane's cook out will probably not do the trick.

The photo is the first step of the profile, the next step that you need to take care of is that of writing your profile itself. Just like everything else mentioned so far attention to detail and a knack for drawing in the eyes of the consumer is a must. This means that every word of your profile should be tailored to captivate the attention of anyone who reads it. This means that you need a dynamic opening paragraph that not only introduces the store but says something about yourself and who you are.

You don't want to write your memoir or anything, it is after all supposed to just be an opening paragraph, but you need to find a way to condense your goals and how it relates to your life in just a few short and concise sentences. It is really not as hard as it sounds, I went to film school and took many course on how to write log lines. Log lines are the two lines that screenwriters use to sell their scripts to Hollywood producers. In just two concise sentences a two hour film is summarized.

For example, do you remember the action packed science fiction film of the 90's starring Will Smith named "Independence Day". The logline that sold this screenplay to producers was simply, "Aliens invade Earth on Independence day." Unbelievable short description but it does describe the main component of the film. So think of the opening lines of your profile like that, with no frills, no additives, but just straight to the point. After all of these basics in profile creation and implementation are covered, really all that you have left to do is to get your merchandise and start stocking up your shop!

And speaking of stock; that actually leads us to the next question, what are some good start-up items to sell on Etsy? Well if you are into the crafty side of things there are some very good start-up items for you to initially tinker with. Believe it or not one of the crafts that never ever go out of style is that of the homemade cup made from clay! Yes, just like you learned to do (how many years ago?) in your Art appreciation class. That homemade pottery cup that has been gathering dust for years could easily be your first promotional item on Etsy. Just be sure to clean that thing out because no one likes to open their ups box to find it full of cobwebs and spiders!

Next on our list of potential first during your tenure as a shopkeeper at Etsy is that of paintings and drawings. If you have an inclination for art, by all means share them with the world! If you have talent in this area there are always immediate buyers for rare and unique pieces of art and who knows, if they like it well enough this could start a whole new career for you all together! What it the new Picasso was discovered through Etsy! Wouldn't that be something? Then again if your version of art consists of stick figures and horrid blobs of paint you might want to skip this one!

Some other good starter items that are all the rage are DIY wallets and handmade handbags. Most women seem to have an undying love of the handbag and even if they have 20 at home there is always a need to expand and seek out more classy and unique bags to put their things in. Men on the other hand have a great penchant for either losing or severely wearing out their wallets, so making a nice solid DIY wallet is an excellent and reliable product to put up on your Etsy account!

Another great item that you can always do something with from beginning to end is that of the printed T-shirt. If you know how to make your own printed T-shirts you are sitting on a veritable gold mine because there is no end to what you can create on the canvas of a blank t-shirt. And since we all where them, there is no end to all of us seeking out that neat, trendy, and often humorous T-shirt. So, if you have great ideas like these, now is the time to share them with the world, as you begin to build your Etsy Empire!

Chapter 3: Developing a Client Base

Having a steady client base is the bread and butter for the traditional merchant and it is also the mainstay of the up and coming Etsy seller as well. But the thing about building a client base with Etsy that makes it truly amazing is the phenomenon of having a "specialized niche" market. This means that you can build a client base rather rapidly by focusing on some very unique details of a product; one seller for example designed prints for "Game of Thrones" and developed a huge fan base because of it.

These highly specialized markets that specifically cater to their consumers are popping up all over the internet due to the web's capacity for "diffused demand". Another marketing term that simply means that when you are dealing with a global platform such as the internet provides, your demand is much more diffused and spread out than it would be in one local region.

Etsy also provides a 24 hour window to monitor the evolution of your sales in real time, this gives you a way to directly monitor the growth of your clientele in any given area. You can see exactly what is purchased and when it is purchased and any immediate trends in buyer behavior.

After a purchase you can further model client tastes through the use of feedback. All Etsy clients are requested to leave feedback about their buying experience, these comments are a direct window into the buying preferences and habits of your clientele and should be of vital importance in shaping how and what you are selling on the site.

Also of vital importance is networking, when you have a repeat customer have them tell a friend, even in the digital age word of is just powerful as it ever was, and now we have many more modes of conveying this word of mouth. One prime example of course is face book, link your face book page to your shop info, and have your customers like you on their face book page, these face book accounts then become essentially giant billboards that millions of people stare at every single day.

The advertising capability of the internet is virtually endless and the more you take advantage of it the better you will sell. So know your clients, know their taste, specifically tailor your products to keep those specifications in mind. And then encourage your clientele to be proactive with their feedback. Once a good repeat client is established, secure further communications with them through such things as social media, partner with them to further demonstrate the efficiency of your products.

Chapter 4: Make more than $1000 dollars a month

To post your items on Etsy you have to spend 20 cents per item. This is the system's required fee to use the service. Whatever the item may be, you must post 20 pennies for each one. This is a cheap service fee in light of the hundreds that would have to be forked over for a brick and mortar physical store just for rent and utilities. In that regard, if done right, it is far more easy to make a quick thousand dollars off Etsy than you would at the corner store.

Another thing to keep in mind while you are first starting your business is to make sure that the price is not only right for the customer but it is right for you. After all you have worked hard on the product and you shouldn't sell yourself short. So come up with prices that are both reasonable for you and your client. You want prices to reflect the reality of supply and demand, because prices that are too low will blow up in your face later when you realize that your profit margin is so narrow you can't even afford to get supplies for the manufacture of new products! So always try to be realistic with your pricing.

Along with adequate price you should also think about building your support base. In the previous chapter we mentioned building a client base, but just as importantly when you start your own business is having good support base. This means quite simply having family and friends that will support you through the thick and thin of what could be a tumultuous first few months of your Etsy start up. In the first few months of your business it is easy to get discouraged, so you need that solid base to keep you going. Everyone get's discouraged but as long as you have the encouragement of those around you and the knowledge that "all good things" take time, you will be in great shape!

The internet is an ocean of opportunity utilizing the resources and needs of 7 billion people on planet Earth, as Etsy has proven there is a lot you can do with this great resource, but at the same time if no one can find your product in that vast ocean of commerce you will not be able to help yourself or anyone else. This is where the importance of key word searches come in. You may not be accustomed to it, but the more refined your key word density, the more easily you will be able to have the right people find the right product.

The basic idea of optimizing key words in search engines, is to take any given product and tag to it a saturation of key words that relate to that product and will pull the item you are selling out of that internet ocean we spoke of and to the surface for prospective buyers to see. For example If you are trying to sell and up cycled couch made from pallet wood you would create tags that reflected that; "couch furniture up cycled pallet reconditioned." This will enhance your chances of getting a solid hit within a buyers search for your product.

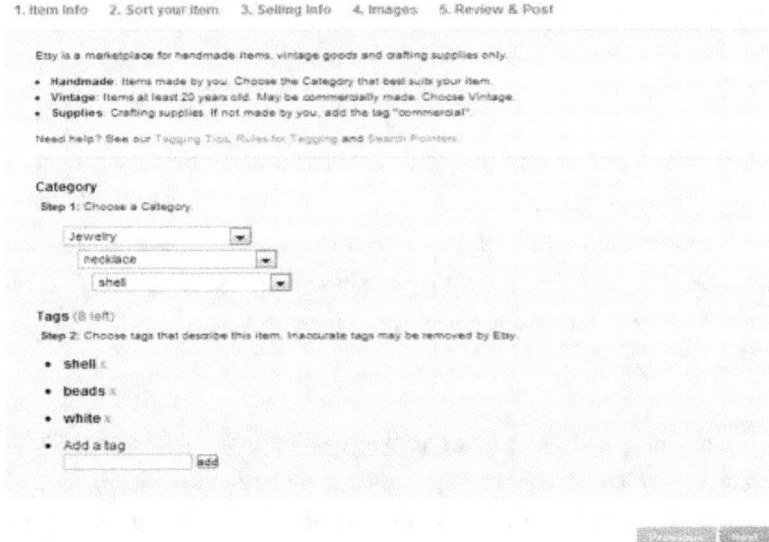

And once the hits start coming in, the money starts coming in. And when you begin to get a residual flow of income from the products you will be more at liberty to start experimenting with special deals and further incentives for your customers. And if one of these gambles pays off keep working with it. For example you could promo your material advertising special gifts or maybe even demo products that incentivize people to buy the product and then at the same time work to advertize other merchandise, this creates a sort of echo effect maximizes your advertizing potential buy selling just a few products.

You can also create special one-time discounts, or offer to pay shipping and handling to get the buyer in the door. Merchants utilize these kind of marketing techniques because they work, when you feel comfortable with your products and your clients, you will be amazed at the positive feedback loop that you have created when you try some of these tried and true marketing strategies out for yourself.

Once you have been successful for a while in the system you will then eventually be selected as a "Featured Seller" on Etsy. This is an additional promotional tool used by the creators of Etsy itself to showcase their top selling shops. Since Etsy takes a small cut of your profits, they also have incentive to promote their best shops. It's really a win win situation where everyone is happy.

If you are happy and content making money off of a vast clientele then Etsy is also happy because you have become an integral part of their own yearly profit margin and as such they will pull out all the stops to further promote you and send you right to the top of the charts!

And as your business is rapidly expanding you will find yourself with an ever growing need to obtain the raw materials for whatever it is that you are producing. As demand for your merchandise grows you will have to find ways to obtain your resources in a cost effective manner. In the pursuit of this developing a good rapport and relationship with a couple of vendors is an absolute must. You need to find someone that you know that is steady and reliable and who will agree to your terms for buying material from them at wholesale price.

In doing this be clear as to what kind of business you run and then hammer our clear and concise terms for how you can buy your needed resource at a discount price, in return for the ease in price agree with this supplier to make them your number one provider of material. Establishing partnerships like this are crucial to economic success very early on, and will allow you to get over the hurdles of cost versus profit, catapulting you well over the $1000 a month range in rapid succession.

Whatever you are selling make up a clear plan of goals and expectations with whoever supplies your needed resource. For example, if you are in the business of knitting sweaters, seek out a large but inexpensive proprietor of yarn and consult with them early on explaining to them as thoroughly as you can what you expect to do with and market the products created from the yarn. Then make an agreement (preferably written) as to how you the sweater vendor will enter into a partnership with your supplier of material.

No matter what it is life is hard if you do it alone, so if you want to reach that $1000 goal developing these business partnerships is crucial. So as your business builds keep and eye out early on for a way to get the most bang for your buck when it comes to your main resource material. All of these components in the end will do wonders to work toward your goal of scraping up profits of over a thousand dollars at the end of each month.

Conclusion: Thoughts on Prometheus

There are many phrases that are floated about in regard to the times that we are living in. We have all heard them, whether it is "digital age" "information age" "communication age" and so on and so forth. There have been more designated titles put forth on the current times that we live in then any other time period. In many ways this age should be called the "Trend age" or the "Niche" decade, because there are so many various trends that are appearing and disappearing on an almost daily basis that it really boggles the mind.

We find it is hard to keep up with the ever changing environment that we live in so many of us have given up entirely and opt instead to just live in the now. This is what a constantly evolving marketing platform like Etsy is all about. It doesn't take a marketing genius and it doesn't take a million dollars to start a lucrative business through a program like Etsy but what it does take is some hard work, determination, creativity and a bit of confidence. Because once you master your own fears and doubts about starting your start-up the sky truly is the limit.

There is no end to what someone can do with a platform such as this. And that was the exact intention when three guys out of Brooklyn New York came up with this peer to peer based buying and selling system. It truly is amazing that just about anyone can sign up for a program like Etsy and then for as little as 20 cents they can start posting their products immediately. The sheer ease with which digital shops can sprout up remind me of when I visited Greece and saw street vendors popping up on every corner, they didn't bother with a license or any other formality they just put up a small wooden stand and sold their gyro's, necklaces or whatever else it was that they had.

And now in the digital marketplace things are working for us practically the same way, you don't need to an attorney to filter out stacks of endless legal paper mumbo jumbo. With just a password and a username you are able to create your own instant access marketplace that can actually pool far more customers than a vendor, even on the busiest street corners of Athens! (Sorry Greek vendor dude!) So this is the great gift that has been bestowed upon us in the digital age, the gift of taking back our destiny and just as when the Titan Prometheus gave the ancient Greek's fire, this gift has all the makings of a monumental revolution in thought and inspiration.

www.ingramcontent.com/pod-product-compliance
Lightning Source LLC
Chambersburg PA
CBHW030109230526
45471CB00003B/1336